GIANT PANDAS

GIANT PANDAS

SANDRA LEE

THE CHILD'S WORLD

Imagine seeing a huge black and white teddy bear come to life! This teddy bear is almost as tall as a full-grown man. It weighs nearly 300 pounds. The bear looks helpless and friendly and likes to do somersaults. Thick fur and a clownlike face make you want to reach out and hug it! Meet one of the world's most loved animals—the giant panda.

The giant panda is such a rare animal, few people have ever seen one, except in photographs. Wild pandas live in the mountains of Tibet and western China. So few giant pandas exist that they are an endangered species. All of these animals may one day disappear from earth, just as the dinosaurs did.

Even if you traveled to where giant pandas live, you might never see one. They live on remote mountains, in thick bamboo forests. Bamboo is a woody, treelike grass with stiff stems. Bamboo forests are so thick that people cannot walk through them. The panda, however, wiggles and crawls between the tightly packed stalks with no problem.

Bamboo is the most important thing in a panda's life. Although pandas also like honey and mushrooms, bamboo is their main source of food. Adults eat enormous amounts of bamboo—about thirty-five pounds daily! The panda spends about sixteen hours of every day eating. Between meals, it naps in hollow trees or bamboo thickets.

Usually, the panda sits while feeding. With its forepaws and large teeth, the panda strips away the bamboo's hard outer fibers and eats the soft inside. Pandas prefer young, tender bamboo sprouts when they can find them.

Pandas have a special "thumb" that helps them pick bamboo stalks. The panda's thumb is actually a large wrist bone. The bone jams bamboo against the panda's fingers. The panda's five fingers have long, sharp claws. Pandas are one of the few large animals that can grip things as tightly as humans can.

Although it can climb trees, the giant panda spends most of its time on the ground. It moves slowly and does not run very fast, even when it's chased. Leopards and wild dogs are the panda's natural enemies. These animals are no match for an adult panda, but they are a threat to panda babies.

Unfortunately, humans are the greatest threat to pandas. Years ago, Asia contained enormous bamboo forests, and pandas could find plenty to eat. But in recent years, people have cleared the forests for lumber and farming.

Also adding to the panda's rarity is the high death rate among cubs. A female panda may give birth to two or three cubs, but rarely does more than one survive. The cubs are so small and helpless that the mother cannot care for more than one. A newborn panda weighs only about five ounces and can be held in a person's hand! The cub cannot crawl until it is three or four months old. The mother panda carries her cub in her jaws if it needs to be moved.

Newborn pandas are covered with very fine hair. Thick black and white fur grows in about three to four months later. A panda's skin is dark under the black fur and pink under the white fur. Though the fur looks soft, actually it is stiff and coarse.

Once it is several months old, a panda cub can get around on its own. It loves to twist and turn. It walks with its toes slightly turned in, waddling from side to side. For play, it likes to roll around in the dirt and climb trees. Young pandas also enjoy sliding down snow-covered hills!

Soon after its first birthday, the young panda leaves its mother. Adult pandas live alone, except to mate. Usually, a panda's territory is about one or two miles across. The panda marks its territory so other pandas will stay away. Marking is done by rubbing the scent glands near its back legs against trees. Sometimes the panda marks a tree while standing on its head!

The giant panda is the most well-known, but not the only kind of panda. There is also the *lesser*, or *red panda*. It lives in the same part of the world as the giant panda and also eats bamboo. Although related, the two pandas look nothing alike. The red panda is much smaller and looks more like a raccoon. The red panda spends most of its time in the trees, coming down only to eat.

The future of the giant panda is uncertain. Very few of them still live in the wild. Some scientists think only about 1,000 wild pandas are left. People of China have set aside land for pandas, and the government has given pandas to zoos throughout the world. Unfortunately, pandas don't breed well in captivity. Groups all over the world are still working to save the panda from extinction. Let's hope they succeed!

INDEX

birth, 20

claws, 15

cubs, 20

enemies, 16, 19

feeding, 12

food, 10

fur, 5, 23, 32

habitat, 9

humans, 15, 19

newborns, 20, 23

play, 25

range, 6

red panda, 29

scent glands, 26

size, 5, 20

skin, 23

sleeping, 10

territories, 26

thumb, 15

walking, 16, 25

zoos, 30

PHOTO RESEARCH
Charles Rotter/Archipelago Productions

PHOTO CREDITS
Ron Kimball: front cover, 4, 18, 24, 31
San Diego Zoo: 2, 14, 22
George B. Schaller: 7, 8, 11, 13, 17, 21, 27
Frank Todd: 28

Library of Congress Cataloging-in-Publication Data
Lee, Sandra.
Giant pandas / by Sandra Lee.
p. cm.
Summary: Describes the physical characteristics,
habits, behavior, and life cycle of the giant panda.
ISBN 1-56766-009-6
1. Giant panda--Juvenile literature. [1. Giant panda.
2. Pandas.] I. Title.
QL737.C214L44   1993   92-35066
599.74'443--dc20

Distributed to schools and libraries in the United States by
ENCYCLOPAEDIA BRITANNICA EDUCATIONAL CORP.
310 South Michigan Avenue
Chicago, Illinois 60604